MICROSEASONS

MICROSEASONS

A Slow-Living Guide to the Year Following the Traditional Japanese Calendar

TIFFANY FRANCIS-BAKER

Hardie Grant

NORTH AMERICA

contents

chapter two: summer   page 48

7: rikka
beginning of summer

19: frogs begin croaking
20: worms wriggle to
the surface
21: bamboo shoots
sprout

8: shōman
lesser fullness

22: silkworms feast on
the mulberry leaves
23: safflowers bloom
in abundance
24: barley ripens,
ready to be harvested

9: bōshu
grain in ear

25: praying mantises
hatch and come forth
26: fireflies fly out from
moist grass
27: plums ripen,
turning yellow

10: geshi
summer solstice

28: prunella flowers
wither
29: irises bloom
30: crow-dipper sprouts

11: shōsho
lesser heat

31: warm winds blow
32: lotuses begin to
bloom
33: young hawks learn
to fly

12: taisho
greater heat

34: paulownia trees
begin to produce seeds
35: the ground is damp,
the air hot and humid
36: heavy rains fall

chapter three: autumn

chapter four: winter

Introduction

Of all the beautiful words in the Japanese language, *kisetsukan* is perhaps the most appropriate for this book. It refers to the concept of being guided by the changing seasons, living in harmony with the natural world, and existing in a way that is emotionally, intellectually, and physically connected to nature's cycles. But in the ancient Japanese calendar, there are more than just four seasons to align yourself with. Spring, summer, autumn, and winter are each divided into six, and each of these 24 subdivisions (*sekki*) are then further divided into three, to make a total of 72 microseasons (*kō*), each lasting around five or six days.

So, what exactly is a season or microseason? This may seem like an obvious question, but the answer is a little more complicated because there are three different ways to classify a season in common use today. The astronomical seasons, for example, are based around the equinoxes and solstices, while the meteorological seasons tend to be divided into periods of three whole months. These are based on average monthly temperatures, with summer as the warmest and winter as the coldest.

The last form of seasonal measurement is known as the phenological season, which is more closely aligned with the Japanese microseason calendar. Here, phenological indicators (phenomena that are correlated with climatic conditions) are used to define the seasonal changes. These include ecological and biological signs like leaves falling from the trees, flowers blossoming in summer, or songbirds calling in spring. These events are influenced by weather and climate, which means they are often more fluid and hard to pin down, but can also be considered a more accurate representation of the ever-changing seasonal patterns as we adapt to the consequences of climate change.

This traditional almanac, which is based on the lunisolar calendar, dates back to the sixth century, when it came to Japan from China via Korea. It was then rewritten and adapted for the Japanese island climate in 1684 by astronomer Shibukawa Shunkai. Each microseason has been translated from the original in slightly different ways, but at the heart is an appreciation of the agricultural and natural cycles, the plants and animals that make up an ecosystem and, in turn, a society.

The exact nature of the microseasons may differ in certain climates, habitats, or landscapes. This does not, however, imply that the meaning behind each microseason cannot be applied to life outside Japan, or even outside the northern hemisphere. The aim of this book is to explore the rich texture and details of the traditional Japanese microseasons and unearth the ideas, symbols, and energies behind each one. We can then take these ideas and combine them with the universal wisdom found within the natural world, and apply what we have learned to our own lives and internal seasons. Most importantly, by studying the microseasons we can form a closer connection with the world around us, encouraging us to think about our impact upon the landscape and our place within a wider, interconnected network, wherever we reside.

In any seasonal calendar, there are no real beginnings or endings, only an ever-turning wheel that rolls forward into an unknowable future, and never back into the past. This is one of the reasons that living more seasonally can be such a powerful tool for moving through the modern world. As a species, many of us have forgotten that we are only animals, and that animals are deeply rooted in the rhythms of nature. Over millions of years, we have evolved to listen to these rhythms, but the chaos of twenty-first century life has warped our sense of order, and now many of us feel tired and burnt out all through the year. As humans, we tend to treat every season (or microseason) more or less the same, rather than aligning ourselves with more instinctive patterns of behavior.

Embracing the microseasonal calendar is one way of observing how the world around us changes. From the first cold mornings of autumn, which send shocks to our system after the long, sunlit days of summer, to the darker nights of winter that invite us to look up at the stars and imagine life beyond our planet, tuning into our surroundings can help us reflect inwardly on our own internal shifts. We have our own bodily rhythms and seasons that can help guide us through the days, weeks, and months—if we only stop to listen. In the microseason calendar, these shifts can be captured in small, bitesize pieces of time that allow us to move steadily through the pace of the year with wonder and joy.

This book is designed as a companion for anyone trying to align their lifestyle more closely with the rhythms of nature. The microseasons can be used as markers and prompts to reflect inward while you look outward. There is no right or wrong way to live more seasonally, but this book should hopefully inform and inspire you to celebrate the microseasons in your own unique way.

As a suggestion, you might like to first work out how closely the microseasons in this book align with the region in which you live. Does your winter coincide with the Japanese winter, for example, or are they reversed? Depending on your preference, you can then follow the microseasons as they unfold throughout the year, or simply dip in and out whenever you need a little seasonal boost. If you are feeling creative and buoyant, for example, you might like to look to the spring microseasons for ideas and inspiration. Or perhaps you are feeling the need to withdraw and look inward, in which case the reflections and practices in the autumn or winter sections might prove more useful.

However you use this book, I hope it brings you closer to the rhythms of the natural world, of which we are all a part. The more comfortably we can coexist with other species and landscapes, the happier, healthier, and more fulfilled we will all be, and the stronger and safer our home planet will become. Nature is the ultimate source of age-old wisdom, with the ability to nurture our modern souls, just as it has nurtured our ancestors for millennia before us.

SPRING

After the long, dark days of winter, there is nothing like a bright spring day to lift the mood. The first shoots creep slowly from the earth, vivid but fragile in their newness, and as each day passes there is more and more greenery against the gray, until all of a sudden the world has erupted back to life. This is the season to appreciate every new leaf and bud, every songbird lining its nest with feathers, every wildflower blossoming beneath the blue sky.

This transitional period between the light and dark halves of the year is also a time to reflect on the balance of nature, the need for rain and sun, frost and thaw in equal measure. Enjoy the feeling of the sun on your skin as you shed your winter coat, but remember to venture slowly into the season of light. The hot summer sun will arrive before long. Do not wish time away. For now, find beauty in the delicate dance of spring: the beat of raindrops against the soil and the hum of honeybees as they feast on new flowers.

1

the east wind melts the thick ice

The signs may be small at first. Hardly noticeable in fact. But if you look carefully, you will see the world beginning to thaw, the landscape slowly awakening from its deep sleep. With the melting of the ice beneath a late winter sun and the first leaves pushing through the soil without ceremony, the subtle scent of change is in the air.

The name of this microseason refers to the power of wind to thaw the winter ice, which is perhaps why symbolically the concept of an "east wind" has come to be associated with change, revolution, and forward progress. The force of the wind keeps the wheel of the year turning and the world moving.

While in your garden or out on a walk, tune into the world as it stirs back to life. Take the time to notice and observe the changing landscape, celebrating each new sign of growth as it appears. Use each of your senses to engage with your surroundings: the sight of early wildflowers; the aroma of thawing soil; the smooth texture of birch buds; the sound of small birds and mammals scuttling among the leaves. Look with new eyes, slow down the pace of life, and notice as much as you can.

2

bush warblers sing in the countryside

The beautiful breeding song of the bush warbler is one of the most celebrated signs of spring, heralding the arrival of warmth and sunlight. The birds themselves are dusky olive brown in color and found all over Japan, from the highest mountains to the densest bamboo thickets.

Now is the time to listen out for birdsong, since many species will spend this season singing their hearts out to attract a mate. Spring is also the best season to enjoy the dawn chorus; an early-morning songbird symphony in which the males sing to defend their territory and find a partner. As dawn breaks, there is generally less background noise from the human world and the air is of a different quality, which means birdsong can be carried up to twenty times farther than later in the day. The females will be eager to find a mate with the strongest voice, since he will be more likely to have the stamina to raise chicks and protect his territory.

Try to identify a few of your favorite birds by their song, which will allow you to listen out for them even as the new spring greenery hides them from view. If you can't bring yourself to leave the house that early, open your window the night before and enjoy the dawn chorus infused with fresh air from the comfort of your own bed.

3

ice cracks, allowing fish to emerge

As the winter ice thaws and the landscape reawakens, now is the time to look for movement amid the stillness. Birds are shifting quietly through the trees, the first buds are bursting slowly into leaf, and the earliest wildflowers are coming into bloom.

Track these signs of movement as they happen, such as the first snowdrop or burst bud, then compare them each year to see if the dates shift over time. Keeping a record will also help you remember what to look out for every year when the long winter feels a little too long. You could track the seasonal changes by writing a simple list or a traditional haiku poem. Alternatively, make a visual record by drawing new leaf and wildflower shapes and keeping them in a special journal. Jot down the date for your own records: you could also make a note of the temperature, the weather, or what you were doing at the time.

HOW TO WRITE A HAIKU

Originating in Japan, a haiku is a short, non-rhyming poem made up of three lines and 17 syllables. Haikus are traditionally themed around nature and seasonal changes, often focusing on a single moment in time, which makes them a wonderful creative tool for capturing the essence of a microseason.

In Japanese, haikus tend to be written as one complete line, but in English they are usually divided into three lines with the following syllables:
Line 1: Five syllables
Line 2: Seven syllables
Line 3: Five syllables

Another characteristic of haiku is the inclusion of at least one *kireji*, translated as "cutting word," which creates a pause or sense of closure. It is not always included, and in English the *kireji* is often represented as a punctuation mark, such as an ellipsis or dash. As an example, here is an English translation of a famous haiku by Matsuo Bashō:
An old silent pond . . .
A frog jumps into the pond,
splash! Silence again.

Try writing your own haiku inspired by a seasonal change or poignant moment you have observed. Brainstorm a few ideas and play with the words on the page before trying to fit them into the three-line structure. If you can, use a *kireji* to mark a contrast or transition between two different images.

4

rain falls, moistening the soil

There is a point between winter and spring where we are tormented with bursts of warm, sunny weather that disappear again behind gray rain clouds, which seem to linger for weeks. Sometimes it feels as if nature is taunting us, but we can try to see the goodness in these often-wet months of spring.

The summer season ahead can bring weeks without water, which means every living thing without access to a faucet (tap) will be dependent on past rainfall that has soaked and oozed into the ground, storing itself up and nurturing the plants and insects at the bottom of the food chain. Find gratitude in these last, necessary weeks of rainfall, and imagine every droplet quenching the landscape, keeping it green and alive.

Did you know that walking in the rain is one of the easiest ways to boost your health? The air itself is cleaner during and after rainfall because as the raindrops fall through the atmosphere, they absorb dozens of microscopic aerosol particles before they reach the ground, naturally removing pollutants like sulfates and soot that we would otherwise breathe in. If you're walking in a green space, the pounding of raindrops against plants, trees, and soil also releases sweet-scented compounds into the air, which is why it often smells so beautiful after a rain shower. Inhaling these compounds has been proven to improve mood and boost respiratory health and immunity.

5

mist lies over the land

The abundance of spring mist is one of the consequences of living through this changeable season, in which the temperatures soar and plummet at will, causing the weather to behave in strange yet beautiful ways.

Mist forms when the air approaches saturation point, when it holds the most water vapor it can before it turns to precipitation. The densest mist or fog happens when the air cools down and advances into warmer, more humid patches of air nearby. The drop in temperature condenses the water vapor and leads to the phenomenon we know as mist, a blanket of gray draped over the landscape, both bewitching and unnerving in its unknowability.

While it may not be ideal for sailing, flying, or driving, it can be a beautiful weather pattern to witness on foot. Take a walk in the spring mist and allow the landscape to reveal itself to you slowly. Even better, visit a place you know well and see how the mist transforms it into somewhere new entirely. Does it feel familiar or hostile? Is it prettier, gloomier, or a bit of both?

HOW TO PHOTOGRAPH
THE MIST

Taking a photo of mist or fog is a great way to capture the atmosphere and interesting light of this strange phenomenon. It is also simple and easy for beginners who are new to the art of photography, as mist makes for a beautiful photographic subject no matter what kind of camera or level of experience you are working with. Here are some tips to help you get started:

- Mount your phone or camera on a tripod to help reduce shaking and blurring.

- Experiment with rays or pockets of light streaming through the mist, particularly around sunrise when it can create magical, haunting, or dreamy effects.

- Make use of interesting shapes or silhouettes in contrast against misty backdrops.

- If your camera has a focus function, try focusing manually rather than automatically, so you can home in on the most interesting details.

- Use a faster shutter speed to freeze the motion of the mist, helping to produce a well-balanced and sharp exposure.

6

trees and plants
put forth buds

**As the bare tree branches begin to erupt with new growth,
look for hope and potential in their leaves and buds.**

The spring rain and rising temperatures will transform the landscape into a luscious, green haven, which makes this time of year one of the best to enjoy forest bathing. A relaxation practice known in Japan as *shinrin-yoku*, forest bathing is a form of meditation that involves being calm and quiet among the trees and breathing deeply to boost your health and well-being.

Head to your nearest woodland area, turn off your devices, and take long, deep breaths. If you can, try to exhale for twice the length of your inhale, as this triggers a relaxation response in the brain. Sit, stand, or lie down quietly and focus on your senses. What can you see, smell, hear, and feel? Try not to focus on everyday thoughts like tasks or emails; instead, let each unwanted thought pass out of your mind and return your attention to the forest around you. Wrap up if it's cold and remain among the trees for as long as you can, building up to the recommended two hours for a fully immersive forest bathing experience.

7

hibernating insects emerge

As the world begins to wake and warm up, insects and other invertebrates will start moving about in search of provisions.

While many insects die off at the end of summer, leaving their eggs and larvae to continue the bloodline the following spring, others spend the winter as adults in a state similar to hibernation. The correct term is actually "diapause" because only warm-blooded animals hibernate in the true sense of the word. Having taken shelter under the soil within log piles, rocks, and leaf litter, as the temperature rises, they emerge into the world once more. Being cold-blooded, they rely on the outside temperature to regulate their own bodies.

As the spring weather sets in, look out for butterflies, bumblebees, and other adult insects searching hungrily for food, water, and future nesting spots. Take time to observe these freshly woken creatures, and follow their lead by easing gently into the awakening world. Now is a good time to practice self-care, checking in on your lifestyle and making sure you are eating well, staying hydrated, and moving your body. Enjoy the chance to stretch and release any tension in your body, knowing there are months of bright, warm weather ahead.

8

peach trees begin to bloom

Spring is the season of fragility. It is easy to feel the warmth of the sun and believe the good times will keep coming, but this season is also about accepting the balance between light and dark, sun and rain, thaw and frost.

Peach trees, with their soft, delicate, honey- and almond-scented blossoms, need a very specific balance to flourish. In order for a peach tree to flower and produce fruit, it first needs to experience a period of chilling, ideally around 500 hours within temperatures between 32 and 50°F (0 and 10°C). This initiates a chemical process within the tree that brings about the flowering buds. Any higher, and the process won't begin; too much colder, and the following year's flower buds may be killed off.

Imagine yourself as a peach tree this spring, recognizing and embracing your own fragility, your own need for light and dark. Consider the idea that life cannot be warm and sunny every day; we need the cold and the dark to grow into the most fruitful versions of ourselves. If you can, find some time to meditate on the idea of balance as spring pushes forward.

9

cabbage whites emerge from their cocoons

Spring brings new life and new beginnings, and what better demonstration than the sight of a cabbage white butterfly emerging in its final form?

Just a few weeks after hatching from an egg, the cabbage white changes from a caterpillar into a butterfly by spinning itself a silk chrysalis, growing wings, and bursting out as soon as the weather is warm and calm. From here, it will rest and dry its wings before taking flight to begin the next stage of its life.

Channel your inner butterfly and meditate on your past, present, and future self. Embrace the journey you have been on to bring you here today, and imagine what kind of person you might become in the weeks, months, and years ahead. What obstacles have you overcome? What are you proud of today? Which mountains would you like to climb and conquer tomorrow? Do not be afraid of change. It is healthy to outgrow our old selves and open our minds and bodies to new adventures. Let go of the things that no longer serve you, and remember that it is never too late to change who you want to be. Your future self will be so grateful for the decisions you make today.

WRITE A LETTER TO YOUR FUTURE SELF

This simple exercise is a wonderful way to focus on who you are today and how you want to grow into the person you will become. There is no right or wrong way to write a letter to yourself, and nobody ever has to see it—even you! If you would like to read it again one day, you might like to seal it in an envelope, labeled with the date you are allowed to open it. Here are a few ideas to help you get started:

- What do you want to remember?

- What would you like to forget?

- What are your favorite things at the moment?

- How are you feeling today, at this exact moment?

- What lessons have you learned recently?

- What would you like to ask your future self?

10

sparrows begin building their nests

The hustle and bustle of spring begins to take over the landscape as birds build their nests in the hope of laying a clutch of healthy eggs.

Not only does this often require elaborate construction and engineering using sticks, lichen, spider silk, bark, and mud, it can also take up to two weeks to complete, depending on the species, weather conditions, and availability of materials. But what an accomplishment! A safe, warm home for a pair of birds, ready to raise their chicks and bring new life into the world.

Take inspiration from the nesting birds and turn your attention to home. Invent your own form of spring cleaning and transform the energy of your living space. Are you happy with the furniture arrangements, the furnishings, the fabrics? Does your home reflect your personality or are you finding it stagnant and outdated? Spring cleaning is also a great way to expend spare energy if you have any. Clear your space of clutter, dust those hard-to-reach bookshelves, hot wash the towels, and scrub that oven; it's amazing how a quick spruce up can make an old space feel brand-new.

11

cherry blossoms begin to bloom

Japan is famous for its beautiful cherry blossom season, known as *hanami* or "flower viewing." It is a celebration of the transient nature of cherry and plum flowers, often lasting only a week or two before fading from the trees.

In modern-day Japan, *hanami* attendees may throw an outdoor party beneath the blossoms, day or night, as well as hanging paper lanterns from the branches. These parties are attended by people of all ages, with the younger attendees often partying into the night. There is even a "cherry blossom front" announced each year by the Japan Meteorological Agency, helping people to know when their local blossoms will appear.

These brief, beautiful *hanami* celebrations are a reminder to enjoy the fleeting beauty of each season of life. Do not waste this moment dreaming of another. Step outside and enjoy the present day, the exact moment you find yourself in. Relish in life's metaphorical blossoms, no matter how long they last or how fast they fall. Try not to worry about endings or beginnings; instead, focus on the here and now by practicing a grounding ritual to root yourself into the earth like a beautiful cherry tree.

HOW TO PRACTICE GROUNDING

Grounding, or earthing, is a therapeutic technique thought to electrically reconnect you to the earth. It is usually practiced by walking barefoot, lying on the ground, or submerging yourself in a body of water. To practice grounding:

1. Find a quiet and safe space outdoors.

2. Take off your shoes and socks. Place your feet on the ground and find a seated or standing position that feels comfortable.

3. Close your eyes and breathe deeply, focusing on alleviating tension from your body with every outward breath.

4. Close your eyes, if preferred, or take this chance to observe your surroundings and notice what you can see, smell, and hear.

5. Imagine drawing strength and energy up from the earth through your feet, just as trees and plants find nourishment through their roots.

12

thunder rumbles far away

Just as the warmer weather begins to lull us into summer—CRASH! The sky is ignited with loud, flashing thunderstorms. They develop when the atmosphere is unstable, and are most common in parts of the world where it is hot and humid.

A thunderstorm can feel frenetic and intense, which is why it is often used in books and movies to create a sense of foreboding or emotional tension. But the reality is that thunder is a natural characteristic of the spring weather, and once the storm has finished, no matter how frightening or intimidating it felt at the time, the air feels clearer, calmer, and more refreshing than before the storm broke.

Sometimes it can feel as if we are the only ones going through a rough patch, but did you know that a lightning strike hits the earth approximately 44 times in a single second? Accept the drama of your own metaphorical thunderstorms, from arguments with friends and bad days in the office, to breakups, hectic school runs, and stressful meetings. Recognize that these storms can make us stronger, clearing the air and helping us see things more clearly.

13

swallows return from the south

In many countries throughout the northern hemisphere, the return of the swallows means the undeniable return of spring. They spend their winters in warmer places farther south, heading back to their summer destinations in the north in order to build nests, reproduce, and enjoy a greater abundance of insects to eat.

The swallows' return is like greeting an old friend, one associated with sunshine, balmy afternoons, and summer warmth. Take their arrival as an invitation to seek out past friends in order to make new memories. Perhaps there is an old university friend you haven't seen in years? Maybe there were other parents you made friends with when your children were younger, and you haven't had a chance to catch up since they started school. Or maybe a good friend moved away and you haven't found time to visit them, yet.

Take this opportunity to give them a call and arrange a catchup, even if it's just a simple dog walk or a cup of coffee. Find out what they have been doing in the time since you last saw each other, and enjoy sharing a moment with someone in real life, rather than flicking through their photos on social media. Make time for good conversation and nurturing old friendships, just as the swallows fly happily back into our lives every spring.

14

wild geese
fly north

Just as the swallows arrive, large flocks of geese leave to fly north, yet another balancing act played out by the natural world.

There are many reasons why birds migrate across the world, but it is usually dictated by the availability of food and breeding grounds, as well as the birds' genetics, daylight hours, and the temperature. Depending on the species, some birds will migrate short distances, sometimes just a hundred miles or so; others can fly for several hundred miles, crossing tempestuous seas and hostile territories to reach their seasonal homes.

As the birds migrate to new pastures and build their nests, take time to reflect on the idea of home. What does a home mean to you? Is it a particular place or space? Is it something that moves from year to year, depending on how you feel? Or is it something that travels inside you, meaning that home is wherever you want to find it?

Whatever your own "nest" looks like, practice gratitude for having a place to eat, sleep, and feel warm, clean, and restful, alone or with friends and family. Can there be anything more nourishing for the soul than stepping into your own private space and finding a home full of comfort?

15

rainbows begin to appear

As Dolly Parton once said: "If you want the rainbow, you gotta put up with the rain." It is only through the careful balance of sunlight and raindrops that we are able to enjoy one of nature's most colorful spectacles.

In most cultures around the world, rainbows are associated with prosperity, hope, and good luck. In Japanese mythology, the *Ame-no-ukihashi* or "Floating Bridge of Heaven" is thought to have been inspired by the rainbow, connecting the earth with heaven and holding the gods Izanagi and Izanami as they made the world out of chaos.

For many, the sight of a rainbow is a good omen, offering hope and new beginnings. The next time you see one appear in the sky, use it to focus on all the positive things that are happening, or may happen soon, in your life. The act of positive thinking has scientifically proven benefits, with optimistic people being more likely to have a better quality of life, higher energy levels, faster recovery from illness, and a longer lifespan. To start thinking more positively, try focusing on the good things in your life, rather than dwelling on the bad. Practice gratitude at least once a day; if you have time, make a note of three things you are grateful for before you go to sleep. You could also try positive self-talk by only speaking to yourself in a way you would speak to others, with kindness and compassion.

16

reeds begin to sprout

The term "reed" can loosely be applied to a number of wetland plants, including grasses, sedges, cattails, and restiads. Not only are they a vibrant component of the landscape, but reeds have also been used for centuries in a number of ways, including to make musical flutes and pipes.

In spring, the regrowth of reeds creates a surge of plant life along the waterways, creating much-needed shelter and habitats for wildlife. As the reeds begin to sprout and emerge, take this as an invitation to surrender to your own creative project. Is there a crafting idea you've had your eye on for a while, but not found the time for? Perhaps you've been wanting to start a nature journal, write the first chapter of a book, or learn a new skill?

Spring is bursting with energy, ready to uplift and inspire if you decide to harness it. What would you like to achieve with that energy? Feel it flowing through you and out through your fingertips, ready to make, draw, craft, or create whatever you're feeling called to.

17

rice seedlings grow

This microseason is often celebrated when the last frosts have finally passed, meaning seedlings and young plants are free from the threat of low temperatures stunting their growth or killing them off completely.

The semi-aquatic rice plant is particularly susceptible to frost, and as Japan alone produces over 7 million metric tons of milled rice a year, it is important to know when the seedlings have the best chance of survival to kickstart the three to four months it takes for rice plants to mature. In the spirit of the season, now is the perfect time to plant your own seeds, nurturing your own source of food in whatever form that might take and observing its progress in the lead up to harvest season later in the year.

Studies have found that gardening and tending to plants has a wide range of mental health benefits, including combating depression, anxiety, stress, and high blood pressure. It doesn't matter if you have an acre of land or a kitchen windowsill; there is always something to grow, and you may be surprised at how fulfilling it can be.

HOW TO GROW FROM SEED OR BULB

You can grow a huge variety of crops at home. Each will require different conditions and care, so you can make choices based on the space you have available:

- Windowsill crops can be grown in medium pots without taking up too much room. Don't forget to pop them in a sunny spot, and remember to water them frequently since they won't have access to rain. Cress, pea shoots, basil, parsley, mint, chives, kale, baby beets (beetroot), and radish can all be grown this way.

- Outdoor container crops include tomatoes, beets (beetroot), carrots, fava (broad) beans, potatoes, arugula (rocket), runner beans, chilies, peppers, scallions (spring onions), and turnips. Perfect for balconies, raised beds, or patio gardens, you don't need acres of greenery to grow these crops. Make sure your containers are full of well-drained, fertile soil to achieve the best results.

- Outdoor ground crops include zucchini, pumpkins, squash, kale, carrots, cauliflower, broccoli, fava beans, chard, spinach, garlic, and onions. If you do have a little more room to spare, experiment with greens, gourds, and other vegetables. Unruly, wide-spreading plants can be trained upward using a teepee made from bamboo canes.

18

peonies bloom

In the language of flowers, peonies are often associated with prosperity, honor, and good fortune. In Japan, tree peonies are admired for their open flower forms, upright growth, and vibrant array of colors.

The peony plant itself has an exceptionally long lifespan, with individual plants sometimes passed down through generations. They can also be propagated, meaning that a single plant can, in some ways, live multiple lifetimes. The flowers, however, have a relatively short blooming period, lasting only seven to ten days. In one way, the peony is a bittersweet reminder of how nothing lasts forever. On the other hand, they also represent longevity and the cyclical rhythms of nature, the eternal loop of growth and decay, death, and rebirth.

As the spring flowers bloom and blossom, find solace in each one, remembering that while no one thing lasts forever, everything is connected eternally. Enjoy each sweet moment you are offered, the highs and lows of life in all its colorful detail. Every moment on earth is a privilege. From the happy days to the sad ones, all are jewels in the treasure chest of life. Find the magic in the mundane and always remember to stop and smell the flowers.

SUMMER

Unlike spring, with its delicate balance between sun and rain, there is no mistaking summer. It is the season of immersion and experience, when the newborn insects, birds, and mammals are more sure of themselves and ready to understand what it means to be alive. Humans, too, often come out of their shells in the summer months. The days are long and balmy, plants and flowers are erupting all around us, and there is something about the better weather that invites us to seek adventure, relaxation, or perhaps something lovely in between.

Whether or not you are a "summer person," seize this moment to capture the energy of the season. As the sun climbs higher and the brightest flowers bloom, relish the chance to dream bigger, broaden your horizons, and absorb the good vibes that summer brings. If big plans aren't a high priority at the moment, then take time out for yourself this season. Soak up the warmth, stay hydrated, look after yourself, and enjoy the experience of watching the world burst into flower, both literally and symbolically.

19

frogs begin croaking

Did you know that in Japan frogs are a symbol of good luck? One of the reasons for this is that the Japanese word for frog, *kaeru*, sounds like the word for "return." Some people see frogs as lucky charms that might bring good things back to them, and travelers have even carried frog charms in their pockets to help them return home safely.

During mating season, male frogs croak loudly to get the attention of females, even if they can't see or hear them. It is hard work and takes a lot of energy, but the rewards are ultimately worth it. In this way, frogs are the ultimate manifesters, calling abundance and fulfillment into existence, and putting in the hard work needed to achieve what they want.

As the frogs begin croaking this microseason, take their voices as an invitation to manifest your own future. Reflect on what might make you feel happy and fulfilled, and begin tuning into the energy of the universe to find a path forward. Then start taking action to make your goals happen. Prepare to work hard like the croaking frogs and understand that, even though we are born into different circumstances, we must all make our own luck. If you want something in this world, you must reach out and shape it yourself.

20

worms wriggle to the surface

Nobody knows exactly why earthworms make their way to the surface of the soil when it rains, although there are many theories. The most popular is that worms find it easier to travel across the top of the soil when it is wet, making it less difficult to find food, places to live, or to reproduce.

When the rain hits the ground, it creates vibrations that call the earthworms out of their underground burrows and up to the top. Birds have been known to mimic these vibrations by drumming their feet against the soil, hoping for a juicy feed.

At this time of year—the liminal space between spring and summer—it can be tempting to wish away the rain and manifest long, dry days full of sunshine. Make the most of these interseasonal moments. Celebrate the warmth and light of the sun, but try not to curse the rain showers as they soak into the soil, giving life and movement to everything they touch.

21

bamboo shoots sprout

Long celebrated as a symbol of strength and prosperity, the versatility of bamboo means it has taken center stage in Japanese culture since ancient times. From edible shoots to paintbrushes, used in papermaking, scaffolding, textiles, and musical instruments, bamboo is celebrated for its quick growth and utility.

In the bamboo groves of Japan the first young shoots spring from the earth and it is time to embrace the eruption of growth as summer's arrival kicks everything into a higher gear. Harness the energy of the earth as it gives birth to new greenery. Let it fizz at the tips of your fingers and toes and fill your lungs with air, as you feel your blood pumping. Start an exercise class you've always had your eye on. Go for a hike somewhere new. Practice a sun salutation on the yoga mat. Stand as tall as a cane of bamboo and feel the energy surge up through you, from the soil toward the sky.

22

silkworms feast on mulberry leaves

The domestic silk moth is one of the main producers of the world's silk supply, made when its larva—the silkworm—continuously eats white mulberry leaves until it is ready to build a silk cocoon. Once harvested, this cocoon can be unraveled to produce one single strand of silk, sometimes reaching almost 3,280ft (1,000m) long!

In order to create this precious strand, silkworms will eat only their favorite leaves from the mulberry tree. They know what they like and they know what they need to produce their fine cocoons, and nothing but the best mulberry leaves will entice them.

Treat your mind and body with kindness, nourishing yourself with the best mulberry leaves for your silkworm soul. If you take care of yourself now, you are more likely to flourish in the future and live a more abundant life. Silkworms begin their lives as small, inconspicuous creatures, and it is only through everyday nourishment that they grow in size and spin their cocoons. Be kind to yourself every day, and listen to what your body needs. Small, simple steps will take you where you want to go.

23

safflowers bloom in abundance

Summer is the season of beauty and abundance, and sometimes this beauty can emerge from the most surprising of places. Do not reserve your admiration for only the sweetest, most delicate flowers; remember that beauty can also be found within thorns and prickles.

Safflowers are fast-growing plants that look like thistles, and in some countries they are even considered a weed. But look again and you cannot fail to admire the safflower's vibrant yellow and orange blooms—so vibrant, in fact, that decorative garlands of safflowers were discovered in the tomb of the pharaoh Tutankhamun.

Plant dyeing is an intricate hobby that can develop into a rare skill, but the simple technique known as *hapa zome*, meaning "leaf dye," is a form of Japanese printmaking that involves "bashing" the color out of plants and onto plain fabric. One of the most beautiful aspects of this kind of dyeing is that the colors will fade over time, symbolizing the transient nature of the seasons. If you happen to nurture a patch of safflowers in your garden, try using this technique on the petals to create bunting in beautiful, warm colors.

HOW TO MAKE
SAFFLOWER BUNTING

You will need:

- Cardboard sheet, big enough to cover one flag of bunting
- Plastic sheet, big enough to cover one flag of bunting
- String of plain, uncolored bunting, preferably cotton or silk
- Handful of safflower heads
- Lump hammer

1. Place the sheet of cardboard on a work surface, or use an outdoor floor space that can withstand a hammer blow. Place one or more flags of bunting on top of the cardboard.

2. Arrange the safflower heads over the bunting, leaving white spaces between to create a visual contrast. Place the next one or two flags over the first ones, on top of the safflower heads.

3. Place the plastic sheet over the top of the fabric, then use your hammer to gently bash the flowers until the juices begin to release onto the fabric.

4. Peel back the plastic and top layer of bunting to reveal your sunny safflower design. Repeat as required and allow the fabric to dry naturally.

5. Steam press the bunting to fix the print.

24

barley ripens, ready to be harvested

Barley, wheat, rye, corn, oats, and other cereal grains are some of the most important foods in the world in terms of feeding the population, but for such vital and nourishing crops, the ears of grain themselves are fairly plain and simple to look at. There are no bright flowers, glossy foliage, or exotic fruits found among the barley fields; the beauty instead lies in the versatility of the crop and its ability to feed so many people and be transformed into so many shapes, textures, and flavors.

Take the ripening barley as an invitation to reap the fruits of your own labors, especially from the past season of your life. Revel in your hard work and determination, making sure to recognize your achievements and the journey you have made. But remember, just as the ripened barley ear can be enjoyed as it is or transformed into something new entirely, the work you have done up to now can continue to drive you forward. Find gratitude for abundance and fruition in your life, but keep the positive energy going if you can. Who knows what your ultimate transformation might be?

25

praying mantises hatch and come forth

With their scythe-like hands, praying mantises are the perfect symbol for the harvest season, especially since, just as the grain transforms from a tiny seed, mantises must also go through a long journey of transformation to reach their final form.

Mating in the autumn, the females lay their eggs within a foamy secretion that hardens into an egg "nursery," keeping them protected through the winter. In spring, they hatch into small, wingless nymphs, which will then go through several molts before maturing into fully formed, breeding adults. It is a long journey, full of obstacles and dangers—although not as dangerous as the poor father's, since once he has mated with the female she will often eat him.

These fascinating, powerful creatures are a beautiful reminder of the balance found in every season. Summer is a time for abundance, but that does not always mean bright flowers and birdsong. Sometimes it can appear more ferocious, more striking, capturing the ruthlessness of Mother Nature as each species continues its ongoing quest to survive and reproduce. It is beautiful in its own way, and a stark reminder to respect the power of the natural world.

HOW TO MAKE A VISION BOARD

Begin your own journey of transformation by manifesting something new into your life, setting a strong intention and believing it will become a reality. Then translate that belief into active steps and hard work to bring it to fruition.

No matter what your goals are, one of the most effective ways to set your initial intention is to make a vision board. In its simplest form a vision board is a visual representation of your goals, usually a poster-sized image you can stick on the wall or set as your computer background in the hope that seeing it every day will help you focus on your dreams. There are no rules for making a vision board, but here are some simple steps to get started:

1. First establish what it is that matters most to you by taking some time to reflect on your values and dreams. Are you focused on a short- or long-term goal? Setting a timescale (a year, five years, ten years from now) makes it easier to track your progress.

2. Start gathering words and images that align with your goal. You could cut out images from old magazines that you paste onto another sheet of paper; create a Pinterest board; or make a digital collage. Focus on images that will give you the most motivation, like a dream home or vacation destination.

3. Put your vision board somewhere you'll see it regularly, such as on the fridge or by the bedroom mirror, or use it as your computer's wallpaper. Don't be afraid to update things if your dreams and visions change.

26

fireflies fly out from moist grass

Fireflies are usually only found in quiet, nature-rich areas around a clean water source, and viewing them can remind us of a simpler time before our lives were flooded with electricity, machinery, and industrial noise. Imagine escaping to the countryside to see the landscape light up with a thousand fireflies after dark, without the interference of artificial light to dilute it?

The emergence of these quiet, glowing creatures is an invitation to make time to slow down and watch the summer season unfold around you. It is easy to get swept away with the long days, short nights, parties, weddings, festivals, and vacations, but remember to enjoy the quiet days too.

Take a moment to sit alone with yourself, breathe deeply, and look closely at the world around you. Think about the gentle, positive aspects of your life and ask: What is bringing you joy at the moment? What are the routine micro-events you look forward to each day? Isn't it an honor and a privilege to feel alive in this moment? Find gratitude in the smallest, simplest things and positivity will continue to unfold around you.

27

plums ripen, turning yellow

Remember how the trees frothed with such beautiful blossoms earlier in the spring? Those blossoms were the beginning of a story that ends with sweet, ripe plums hanging from their branches.

The story never ends, of course. The stones hidden inside those plums may fall onto the ground and grow into new plum trees, which will blossom and form fruits of their own, an endless cycle that is reassuring in its consistency. Enjoy the fresh plums in their current form and meditate on the journey they made to arrive here. Which insects pollinated the blossom? Which earthworms enriched the soil at the tree's roots? Which rays of sunlight shone against the leaves? And which raindrops fell against the earth, ready to be soaked up and stored in the flesh of a juicy new plum?

Life is a miracle, a game of chance, and you don't have to look farther than a summer plum to appreciate the wonder of nature's eternal rhythms, of which we are all a part. How comforting is that?

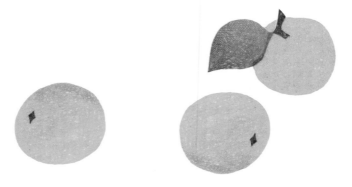

HOW TO SOAK UP THE SEASON WITH ALL FIVE OF YOUR SENSES

- What colors, shapes, textures, and movements can you see around you? What are your eyes drawn to? Which sights fill you with joy and which make you want to turn away? Can you find patterns and repetitions? How does the array of summer colors make you feel?

- Which sounds are constant throughout the day, and which come and go at different times? Do you prefer manmade sounds or those of nature, like birdsong and insects? If you close your eyes, are there any background sounds you didn't even realize were there until now?

- If you inhale deeply, what can you detect on the wind? The aroma of flowers blossoming, cut grass, or food cooking? Or something less pleasant, like car fumes? Which smells make you feel calm and relaxed? How do the indoors and outdoors smell different?

- Can you find new textures to experience? How does the bark of a tree feel, or the softness of summer leaves? Take your shoes off and walk across the grass. Do you feel warm or cold? Grounded or ethereal? How does the warmth of the sun feel on your skin?

- Are you savoring the flavors of the season? Which foods are available in your local area? Which fruits taste sweet, succulent, or sour? Which vegetables are at their freshest and crispest?

28

prunella flowers wither

A traditional plant in herbal medicine, the *Prunella* flower (also known as common self-heal, heal-all, and woundwort) blooms in December, around the winter solstice, and dies off six months later, around the summer solstice.

It is a beautiful reminder of the light and dark halves of the year, especially on the summer solstice, the longest day of the year when there are the most hours of daylight. After this day, the nights start to lengthen again as the earth tips back into balance, calling in the autumn and winter months ahead.

Even in the midst of summer we are reminded of the delicate dance between light and dark, heat and cold, life and death. The withering *Prunella* flowers help us appreciate the seasons in all their shades and textures, gently reminding us that the wheel of the year continues to turn.

HOW TO CELEBRATE THE SUMMER SOLSTICE

- Wake up at sunrise and enjoy every moment of the longest day of the year. Listen to the birds singing and feel the cold dew against the grass. Breathe in the fresh air of the morning and watch the world come to life.

- Stretch your body with a gentle walk or a sun salutation. Feel the energy of the day moving through your fingers and toes, waking up every bone and muscle as the summer sun shines against your skin.

- Eat breakfast outside and savor every mouthful. Sip hot coffee and enjoy fresh pastries, seasonal fruit, or nourishing oats and grains.

- Ground yourself by stepping out onto the grass in bare feet. Stand tall like a tree and feel yourself become rooted into the soil, soaking up its energy and feeling the power of the earth as it lifts you up into a new day.

- Watch the sunset on the longest day and enjoy seeing the sun's long journey to completion. Observe the color of the sky shifting through blue, pink, purple, and orange. Watch the birds making the most of the last minutes of daylight and look out for bats as they begin their crepuscular hunt.

29

irises bloom

The water iris (*Iris ensata*)—often found growing around rice fields since it thrives in aquatic conditions—is one of the most celebrated of the many iris varieties in Japanese art and culture. The flower appears in midsummer, bluish purple in shade with a flash of yellow on the autumn petals.

These beautiful, highly prized flowers thrive in the midsummer sun, but their water-loving nature is also a gentle invitation to balance sunlight with hydration. As the iris blooms, remember to keep yourself hydrated by drinking plenty of fresh water through the summer season, fueling your mind and body as you explore another beautiful phase of life on earth.

If you don't like drinking plain water, try experimenting with iced tea, popsicles, straw cups, or water infused with slices of fresh fruit. Grab a jug of fresh water and add a few slices of cucumber, a handful of summer berries, and a large sprig of mint leaves. Swirl the jug gently to get the flavors going. Leave it in the fridge overnight for a delicious cold drink to enjoy next day.

30

crow-dipper sprouts

The crow-dipper plant (*Pinellia ternata*), commonly known as the peace lily or green dragon, sprouts from the earth around the time of *Hangesho*, a time of rest for the farming community to mark the end of the busy rice-planting season. Traditionally, many people would avoid eating meat or drinking alcohol during this period, giving their bodies the time and energy to recover from the intense planting process of the last few weeks and months.

In this busy, chaotic world, it can be challenging to find the time and space to rest—and it can be even harder to allow ourselves to do so. We are often conditioned to think we must be busy and productive at all times, but this is not true. We can only be the best versions of ourselves if we allow our minds and bodies to recuperate, not just by having a good night's sleep, but by finding pockets of time throughout the day to simply sit and be still, or to enjoy gentle hobbies or activities that fill us with joy and serenity. If you can, find time to rest and replenish your energy stores without feeling guilty.

A RESTFUL MEDITATION VISUALIZATION

Visualization is a form of meditation that engages your imagination and helps relax the mind and body. It is a great way to clear away the clutter of the day and practice "seeing" the world with all of your senses. Try this one to get started:

1. Find a quiet place where you can sit or lie comfortably and relax without being disturbed.

2. Close your eyes and imagine in your mind a peaceful and relaxing place. It could be somewhere real, like your favorite beach or green space, or it could be completely imaginary, like a pool in the middle of a luscious rainforest.

3. Allow your mind to feel and see everything in this place, engaging all of your senses. Listen to the waves lapping the shore, feel the warm sun on your skin, smell the damp earth.

4. If stressful or mundane thoughts drift into your mind, simply acknowledge them, dismiss them, and allow them to drift back out again.

5. Try to spend at least 10 minutes enjoying this visualization if you can, although the longer you can relax and engage with it, the better you are likely to feel.

31

warm winds blow

From the smallest breeze to the most violent tornado, the wind has the power to drive big changes. It can disperse seeds and pollen, helping new plants to grow, or it can rip ancient trees from their roots and open up new spaces. The wind is transformative, clearing debris and clutter, keeping the world moving and growing.

What can the symbolic power of the wind do for you? Is it pushing you in a new direction, or is it easing you gently along your path, guiding you toward a brighter future? Think about your current lifestyle and reflect on the things you love and the things you might like to change.

Are you happy in your chosen career, for example, or are you at the bottom of a ladder you don't really want to climb? Are you pursuing something that reflects your skills and interests? Is your career part of your identity? Or is work something that enables you to pursue other interests?

Do you look forward to social occasions, or are there one or two toxic people you try to avoid? Do your relationships bring out your best side, or turn you into someone you don't like? Do you give to others as much as you receive?

Perhaps there is something you have been wanting to try for years, but never found the time? Are you waiting for the perfect moment or finding excuses to start? Are you worried you might fail, or are you willing to try it and see?

32

lotuses begin to bloom

In the Buddhist tradition the sacred lotus is a symbol of strength, resilience, and rebirth. They grow in muddy, murky waters but rise to the surface and bloom every morning without staining their beautiful, pale petals. Because of this, the lotus has come to represent the enlightened mind rising from suffering and darkness, and because it is rooted in mud, it also symbolizes being unattached to the material world.

In Hinduism, the lotus represents beauty, fertility, purity, and prosperity; it is said there is a lotus flower in the heart of every Hindu, which blooms when they finally achieve enlightenment.

As the summer lotuses begin to bloom, meditate on themes of strength, resilience, and rebirth. Which sources of strength do you draw from when you need support? Do you find resilience inside your own head and heart, or do you look to loved ones to help and guide you? What makes you feel strong and powerful? How could you work toward a more elevated, vibrant version of yourself? What does progress and development mean to you?

Sit with your thoughts, write them down in a journal, and imagine the lotus flower opening in your mind, body, and soul.

HOW TO MAKE A LOTUS MUDRA

The word *mudra*, meaning "seal," "mark," or "gesture" in Sanskrit, usually refers to a hand gesture performed during yoga or meditation practice that is thought to enhance the flow of energy. This lotus mudra is said to open the heart center, releasing the energetic qualities of compassion, forgiveness, and kindness.

You can practice this simple gesture at any time by first sitting comfortably and taking a few deep breaths. To form the lotus shape, bring the base of your palms together near your heart center with your two thumbs gently pressed together and touching your chest. Touch your two pinky fingers together and spread the index finger, middle, and ring fingers wide like a lotus flower opening. Each finger should stand wide apart from the others without touching. Keep this gesture open while you enjoy a few deep breaths, then relax the fingers and place them gently on your thighs to end.

33

young hawks
learn to fly

A young hawk is known as a fledgling once it has developed its first set of flight feathers and learned to fly short distances, but while it grows bigger and stronger, it must remember to return to the nest, or it will leap into the adult world without the skills required to survive.

Engage with your inner fledgling and take flight! Shake off those brand-new feathers, look to the sky, and launch yourself into a new project, place, or experience, trusting in yourself to navigate a new adventure. But remember, it is a good thing to depend on others from time to time, especially if you are fortunate enough to have a loving community of people cheering you on. Seek guidance and wisdom from those who have always been there for you, and don't be afraid to ask for advice, even as you jump the nest and find independence.

True wisdom comes from observation and understanding, and your friends and family will always be there to help you cope with new challenges and celebrate new achievements. It is a wonderful thing to find your own way in the world and make your own mark, but the journey is even sweeter when you take your loved ones with you for the ride.

34

paulownia trees begin to produce seeds

One of the fastest-growing trees in the world, the paulownia tree is known for its ability to produce as many as 20 million tiny seeds in a single year. Each of these is full of potential, bursting with the possibility of growing into a new paulownia tree, and even though the probability of each one succeeding is low, it doesn't stop them all spreading themselves as far and wide as they can.

It is amazing what one tiny seed can do, just as one tiny action can be incredibly powerful. A small act of kindness is the term given to little moments or actions that push positivity into the world, even if they are over in a second or we don't see the consequences of what we do. Giving loose change to a homeless person, smiling at a stranger, saying hello to an elderly person on their own, or even moving a hedgehog away from a busy road. We can never predict how far the ripples of our good deeds might spread. Find meaning and joy by spreading your own small seeds of positivity, taking action every day to make the world a kinder, more thoughtful place.

35

the ground is damp, the air hot and humid

Get ready to harness the last moments of charged summer energy before the season begins to turn. Move your body, visit exciting places, make special memories, and spend time with friends beneath the warm sun.

The name of this microseason refers to the charged atmosphere of late summer, when one minute the sun is shining hot and bright, and the next, humidity and temperatures rise until the sky breaks into thunder and rainfall, soaking the ground with life-giving water. It is a celebration of the dynamism and changeability of the season, and a gentle reminder that the world is rarely predictable.

Now is the perfect time to expend any last surges of energy before the approach of autumn, when we begin to turn inward and slow everything down. Be brave and seek out beauty and brilliance in the world!

36

heavy rains fall

Release a breath. Let your shoulders relax, your neck muscles loosen, your jaw unclench. These are the last days of summer, and although the good weather may linger, there is a shift in the air.

As autumn approaches, this is the time to turn inward. We may mourn the loss of sunshine and warm temperatures, but there is so much beauty in the turn of the season. Autumn invites rest and recuperation, shelter from the intense heat and a chance to look inward, to retreat into our minds and process our thoughts.

As the rains fall on the last moments of summer, extinguishing the heat of the season, take comfort in the relief of autumn's approach. Feel the cool and damp of the earth, full of life and decay, stirring and swirling beneath your feet. Watch the first leaves change color and fall to the ground, creating a carpet of movement and texture. Feel the wind against your skin as it begins, slowly, to cool. Prepare to replenish your store of energy, soothed by the temperate nature of early autumn and encouraged by the last, jubilant rays of the summer sun. It's time to embrace a new season!

HOW TO EMBRACE NEWNESS

If you can feel the effervescence of late summer bubbling up
but you're not sure where to direct it, try some of these ideas for
taking small adventures:

- Find a new walking route in your local area and go for a hike
  with a friend. Bring snacks, enjoy the great outdoors, and take
  the opportunity for a good catchup, all while exploring new
  territory and beautiful scenery.

- Cook with new ingredients and see what you can rustle up.
  You could pick something strange or exotic and research how
  to prepare it; or choose a cuisine from a country you've always
  wanted to visit; or try a cookery challenge with a friend to see
  who can create the tastiest dish.

- Visit a local landmark you've never visited. Do you know how
  many Londoners have never visited the Tower of London?
  Find a special place near you and make time to visit, seeing it
  through the perspective of a tourist and learning something
  new about your local area.

- Experiment with new genres of books, film, or television
  shows. Pick something you wouldn't usually go for and
  embrace it with open arms. Usually watch science-fiction
  movies? Try a war epic or romantic comedy and see what you
  think. Better yet, recruit a friend or loved one and take turns
  to pick from different genres.

- Wear a new color you wouldn't usually wear. It doesn't have
  to be anything expensive—just head to your local thrift store
  and pick out something you wouldn't normally be drawn to.
  If you're into dark, sultry tones, experiment with bright floral
  patterns and see how that makes you feel.

AUTUMN

As the last days of summer fade away, autumn arrives and invites us to slow things down, look inward, and take a deep breath. This is the time to retreat and replenish your mind, body, and soul. Embrace the shift into semi-hibernation and cast off the pressure to be overly busy. Allow yourself more moments of indulgence and self-care, if you can, as we slip gently into the darker half of the year.

Autumn is the time to celebrate endings as well as beginnings. It is a season of harvest, gratitude and balance, a time to take stock of the past few months and give thanks to the earth, to our friends and family, and to look ahead to the long months of winter with lightness and clarity. Incubate the seeds of new ideas, and just as the trees drop their leaves and fruits, let your energy fall back to your roots to form compost for the mind and body.

37

cool winds blow

Take a step back and allow the change of season to wash over you. There is a freshness in the air and a dip in temperature that means the darker half of the year is approaching. This is a wonderful point in time, as it marks the season of rest and replenishment.

In the natural world, leaves will begin to fall from the trees and animals will slow down, ready to get cozy and survive the long, winter months. Embrace the chance to rest and reset, focusing inward with peaceful, calming rituals.

Compile a reading list of favorite novels, history tomes, murder mysteries, illustrated coffee-table books, autobiographies, or poems—anything to keep you company as the nights begin to draw in. You could even start a journal documenting ideas and notes from your reading adventures.

Go for a slow walk in the great outdoors, taking time to notice the changing colors of the leaves, the texture of the earth underfoot, and the smells and sounds of the landscape as summer shifts into fall and the cool winds blow around you.

Meditate with a candle as the evenings begin to grow darker. Choose a favorite scent, or keep it natural with unscented wax, and enjoy watching the flame dance and sway. As you do so, reflect on your mood and emotions, current events in your personal life, or your friendships and relationships.

38

evening cicadas begin to sing

The evening cicada is known for its shrill, deafening call heard in the mornings and evenings of late summer and early autumn.

Cicadas "sing" most often at twilight, when the temperature has dropped, making them a historic symbol of autumn's arrival as the last hot days of summer fade away. For this reason, the evening cicada is a beautiful focal point for reflection on the concepts of life and death, particularly in the autumn season when the landscape itself appears to die away, ready to come back to life again the following spring.

If you can, find time to meditate on the cycle of life, death, and rebirth. Seeing the beauty in nature's rhythms helps you recognize that nothing truly dies; it only changes from one form to another. A plant grows from a single seed, ripening into lush foliage and plump fruits, which then produce their own seeds before rotting back into the earth. Nothing wasted, nothing lost; only the infinite potential of a single seed to return again and again. As the natural world enters its own phase of ripeness, rotting, and rebirth, find reassurance in these eternal, rhythmic cycles.

HOW TO EMBRACE THE SEASON OF RIPENESS, ROT, AND REINCARNATION

Place an apple, banana, or other piece of fruit in an outdoor space, somewhere you can look at it almost every day. This could be your own garden or somewhere public that is tucked away out of sight.

Make time to observe this piece of fruit as it moves through the season, becoming moldy, rotten, or mushy at first before sinking into the earth to start the cycle again, or perhaps disappearing more quickly as it is eaten by insects, birds, or mammals.

Enjoy watching this slow process and reflect on the transience of life, celebrating the fact that we all change form throughout our lives and beyond.

39

thick fog blankets the land

A mist of tiny water droplets sweeps over the land, quenching its thirst after the long, hot summer. The thick, autumn fog is a powerful, cleansing force. It may dampen the spirits after the heat of the sun, but fog has a beauty of its own and can transform the world into a magical and curious place. It can also hide our surroundings, making us feel uneasy in a space with which we were once familiar.

Do not fear changes at this time of year, since they mark the turn of the year's wheel and the eternal onward energy that drives us forward. Instead, allow the fog to calm and cleanse your mind, body, and soul.

Embrace the more subdued energy of autumn and feel the freshness of the changing season. Reflect on aspects of your life you might like to change, and celebrate the fact that we must all shed our skins from time to time, growing and changing as the seasons shift around us. It is an opportunity to look inward and improve our lives, but first we must clear away old energies, people, and possessions that no longer serve us.

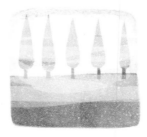

HOW TO PRACTICE CONTRAST WATER THERAPY

As this microseason celebrates the cleansing power of water in droplet form, this is the perfect time to invigorate the mind, body, and soul with the practice of contrast water therapy. Put simply, this means rapidly alternating between hot water and cold water immersions. It is thought this alternation helps to open and close the blood vessels, boosting circulation, reducing fatigue, and easing muscle soreness. Contrast water therapy can easily be practiced at home using the steps below, but always check with a medical professional if you are unsure if it is suitable for you.

The easiest way to practice contrast water therapy is to alternate between hot and cold water in your home shower or bathtub. The cold water should be 50–59°F (10–15°C) and the hot water should be 95–113°F (35–45°C). Start by taking a warm shower, then drop the temperature gradually after a few minutes. If you have a separate bathtub and shower, try running a bath for one temperature and hopping into the shower for the other. If you're feeling particularly bold, try adding ice to your bathtub and staying submerged for several minutes.

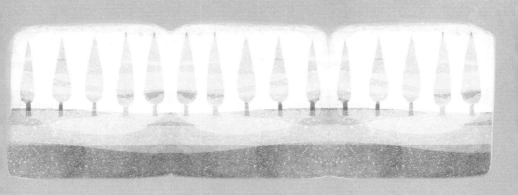

40

cotton bolls open

It takes a specific set of conditions for the round, fluffy cotton bolls to form around the seeds of the plant, including a long period of frost-free temperatures, plenty of sunshine, and a moderate amount of rain. But the result is worth the wait, as each boll is harvested and spun into a soft, breathable thread that has become the most widely used fabric in modern society.

What can we learn from the humble cotton boll? Perhaps that positive things can sometimes take time to develop, and it can be easy to take that journey for granted. Reflect on the positive elements of your life at this moment and take a journey backward, identifying all the hard work and positive energy that was poured into them along the way. Perhaps you are in a strong, loving relationship that took a little effort in its early days? Or perhaps you found your current job incredibly difficult at the beginning, but through perseverance you are now fulfilled and challenged in the best way?

Give yourself credit for the things you have done to bring positivity into your life, and don't forget what it took to get here.

41

the heat finally relents

As the warm weather cools and the autumn season moves in, embrace the fresh air and nourishing winds of change.

Take this time to seek out simple, modest comforts, the sort of rituals and actions that we may have taken for granted in the hullabaloo of summer. Slow down the pace of your day if you can and be more mindful in the everyday routines that make up your waking hours.

HOW TO MAKE THE MOST
OF THIS MICROSEASON

- Enjoy the ritualistic process of making a cup of tea or coffee. Watch as steam fills the air, the water darkens in the cup as the tea leaves or coffee grounds infuse, and the milk splashes into the liquid for that dash of sweet creaminess. Savor the taste as it cools, avoid picking up your phone, and instead give yourself five minutes to gather your thoughts and feel refreshed before the day continues.

- Find time to sort through your closet and change a few things around as colder weather approaches. Pack away the summer T-shirts and flip-flops and bring your coziest sweaters and scarves to the front of the shelf.

- Even if the weather turns, try and get out for a walk once a day. The fresh air and exercise will boost your mood. If possible, avoid plugging in music or a podcast. Instead, tune into the sounds around you, from the melodies of autumn birdsong to the distant roar of a plane.

- Although this is the perfect time of year to slow down, remember to keep your body limber with gentle movements, even if it is just a five-minute stretch first thing in the morning and last thing at night. Listen to your body and enjoy feeling alive within it, celebrating the rhythms of your inhales and exhales, your blood pumping, and your muscles contracting and relaxing.

42

rice ripens

In Japan, this microseason encompasses *Nihyaku-toka* (translated as "210 days") on September 1st, a date that marks 210 days since the start of spring, as well as the start of the typhoon season.

Typhoons can be devastating to staple crops like rice, which is just beginning to ripen in time for the harvest after a long growing season. The heavy rain and strong winds can destroy them all before they are harvested, wiping out an entire crop in one stormy period. According to legend, the astronomer Shibukawa Harumi, who originally recorded the Japanese microseasons in 1685, woke up on the first day of September and decided to go fishing, but was warned against it by the boatman who told him the weather always took a bad turn on this fateful day. Choosing to go anyway, the skies quickly darkened and a storm rolled in. When he returned to the shore, he marked the day in his calendar and declared *Nihyaku-toka* an "unlucky" time of the year. In fact, *Nihyaku-toka* has become so ingrained in Japanese culture that in 1960 the government designated September 1st as Disaster Prevention Day. Local governments often use this date to practice emergency drills against natural disasters like earthquakes.

While we should avoid being overly worried or anxious about our day-to-day lives, take this opportunity to reflect on anything that is making you feel a little unsettled.

HOW TO KEEP YOUR INTERNAL STORMS IN CHECK

Perhaps there are issues in your close family or friendship circle, you are worried about your health, or global events are making you feel increasingly anxious. Is there anything you can do to alleviate these worries? If so, get them out of your head by writing them down and thinking about them clearly.

Make a realistic, long-term plan to remove unnecessary worries from your mind. If they cannot be removed, try to find acceptance instead of allowing them to take center stage in your life.

43

white dew shimmers on the grass

A dewdrop is usually formed on an object that doesn't easily conduct heat. As the object quickly cools, this causes water vapor to condense into droplets on its surface. They are formed in a short space of time and disappear just as quickly, as soon as the morning sun shines and turns them back into water vapor to continue their eternal circulation through the atmosphere.

In Japanese literature, dew has become a symbol of autumn and the fleeting nature of life on earth. This is not a negative outlook, but a celebration that life and death are connected in an everlasting circle. In every aspect of the natural world, and especially in our human lives, there are no real endings—only miraculous transformations from one form of energy to another.

Autumn is a time of death and decay in the natural world, as leaves fall and insects die before the long, hard winter. But remember that there is beauty in every part of the natural cycle, including in death, when plants and animals return to the soil, ready to take on new life in the spring.

44

wagtails begin to sing

The wagtail is usually found near water bodies such as streams, rivers, and lakes. In Japan, it features in the creation myths of the indigenous Ainu people of northern Japan.

One story describes how the great creator sent a "water wagtail" to create the first banks of land in the watery world beneath. The wagtail flew down and splashed the water aside before packing the earth firm with its feet and beating it with its tail, creating the Ainu islands in the process.

As autumn creeps in, this is the perfect time to channel your inner wagtail and embrace the watery weather in all its forms, from the lightest drizzle to the most tempestuous storms. Find gratitude for the rainy season and celebrate the life-giving properties of the water cycle.

HOW TO ENJOY THE RAIN

- How does the old saying go? There is no such thing as bad weather, only bad clothing. Grab your finest waterproofs and head out into the rain for a refreshing walk.

- Making water art is fun to try with children. Take a piece of paper and draw a few patterns over it in your favorite, brightest colors. Then leave the paper out in the rain and watch as the raindrops transform it into a swirly, abstract masterpiece.

- If you have a conservatory or large window, there is nothing more soothing than listening to the rain. If you don't, try experimenting by placing something metallic, such as a baking tray or saucepan, outside, and see how the rain sounds against its surface.

- Tiny creatures like slugs, worms, and snails love the rain, so a shower is the perfect time to have a look around your local area to see what you can find. Not all slugs are brown and boring, so look out for interesting patterns, colors, and textures.

- Remember disposable cameras? They are still available to buy, and a waterproof one can produce a range of fun, watery photos full of movement and memory.

45

swallows return to the south

The swallows have finished their summer vacation and will now return to warmer climates in search of food and shelter. They will be missed, but it is reassuring to know that in just a few months' time, they will reappear once again.

Take comfort from the swallows' journey and celebrate the ebb and flow of the natural world. Beginnings lead to endings, but endings, in turn, lead to new beginnings.

Reflect on your own beginnings and endings over the last year, whether they are positive or negative. Has something or someone disappeared from your life who you long to see again? Can you find a way to create something new from the situation, just as a phoenix rises from the ashes? Or is there something that has reached a natural end in your life? Something to which you will be happy to bid farewell and move forward? Celebrate your beginnings and endings in all their forms, from the saddest departure to the happiest new start.

CLEANSING WITH INCENSE

The practice of burning incense for cleansing and purification purposes has existed in many cultures for centuries. When burned, incense releases a fragrant smoke that can help concentrate thoughts and intentions, as well as dispelling negative energy and bringing positive energy into your space.

If you are new to burning incense, begin by mindfully setting your intention for the energy cleansing process, then light your incense stick or bundle using a candle, match, or lighter. Allow the flame to catch before gently blowing it out, then allow the incense to gently smolder. If you are unsure which fragrance to choose, sandalwood, lavender, rose, and kasturi are all known for their positive, purifying properties.

46

thunder comes to an end

The heightened drama of the summer season, marked by intense heat, loud, rolling thunderstorms, and high humidity, will now make way for the calm and tranquility of autumn. Look back on the last few months of activity and excitement with fondness, but embrace the new season ahead, which will offer you a chance to rest and recuperate, to be still and look inward upon your own thoughts and ideas.

Enjoy the magic of silence and solitude. Meditate on new projects and ideas but allow yourself time to nurture them before jumping into action. Plant seeds in your mind for your future life, but let them sink into the soil of your soul, so they may germinate and grow over the months ahead.

Experiment with enjoying as much silence as you can. Try to resist music and podcasts for a little while, and instead listen to the whirr of your own thoughts as they churn and percolate. Respect the smallest, quietest voices at the back of your mind. What are they trying to tell you? Do not be afraid to be alone with your thoughts, and never underestimate the wisdom of your own mind when you choose to listen to it.

47

insects close up their burrows

At this time of year a number of insects will be preparing for the long, dark winter ahead by snuggling down into their burrows and closing up the entrance to keep themselves safe and warm. We can learn a lot from these cozy creatures, especially as we will likely be spending more time in our own homes as the nights draw in and the temperatures drop.

Celebrate the season of hibernation by preparing your own hibernaculum, a place for you to seek shelter during the darker half of the year. Clean and declutter if you can, and make your nest, den, or burrow as comforting and cozy as it can be.

HOW TO REFRESH YOUR HIBERNACULUM

- While the temperature is still above zero, open the windows wide and allow the fresh air to blast through your home.

- You know those crevices that never see the light of day? The bottom drawer of the fridge, the underside of the sofa cushions, the dishwasher filter—all the places you ignore through the year? Indulge in a bit of deep-cleaning and see how much fresher it makes everything feel.

- We can all be guilty of hoarding too many trinkets, unworn clothes, and unread books, so treat yourself to a ruthless declutter and find new homes for the things that don't bring you joy.

- Knitted throws, scented candles, soft cushions, and fresh coffee; make sure you are fully stocked for the season ahead with all your favorite home comforts, ready for those cold, dark mornings and long evenings.

- If you're feeling stagnant and unenthusiastic about spending more time at home, try rearranging a few pieces of furniture in your main living spaces. A few simple moves can make a home feel brand-new, as well as making the best use of the space and layout you already have.

48

rice paddies are drained of water

Part of the practice of farming rice involves the careful management of the rice fields (paddies), since crops need to be flooded in specific amounts of water at different stages of their growing cycle. Toward the end of the season, when the crops are more mature, the paddies are drained of water in anticipation of the final harvest.

The harvest season in the agricultural world is a time of celebration and gratitude, as the fruits of the last few months' labors are gathered and the feasting table is laden with produce. What more could we need to get us through the long, hard winter than a cornucopia of fresh, delicious food?

Celebrate your own harvest season by reflecting on your achievements this year. Think positively about your own thoughts and actions, and give yourself credit for all the hard work you have put into different areas of your life, whether you're raising a child, learning a new skill, or navigating a new challenge in your career. Find gratitude for the successes you have enjoyed this year, and recognize your own actions in bringing those successes to fruition.

HOW TO HOST A SLOW SUPPER CLUB

One of the simplest ways to celebrate the changing seasons is to host a slow supper club at home. The focus should be on delicious food, great conversation, joyful moments, and a chance to slow down and appreciate the year as it unfolds around you.

Start by inviting a small, intimate group of friends you love and trust, the kind of people who make you think differently and laugh out loud. Choose a menu of simple, seasonal food like slow-roasted vegetables, locally sourced meat and dairy, a tasty homemade pudding to finish, and a selection of drinks to complement the meal. You could also ask everyone to bring something to contribute in a "pot luck" dinner, which takes the pressure off you as the host and encourages a variety of different food and drink.

For the finishing touch, decorate the table with simple, rustic items found in the natural world, like sprigs of greenery, branches wrapped in fairy lights, or a pitcher of fresh flowers.

49

wild geese begin
to fly back

Birds such as the white-fronted goose migrate back home from their summer residence, arriving in late September and early October to spend the winter in marshes or rice paddies.

These geese will often pair for life, migrating with their mates, siblings, and offspring and forging strong family bonds in the process. They serve as an important reminder to cherish our close friends and family, nurturing the bonds that keep us together and keeping our connections alive no matter what stage of life we find ourselves in.

Embrace your inner wild goose and take this opportunity to spend time with friends and family. Invite them into your home if you have the ability, welcoming them with good food and conversation, and letting them know that you love and value their company. Outside the home, suggest meeting up with loved ones for cake and a coffee, a walk in your local green space, or you could visit a place that you would both enjoy, such as a museum or art exhibition inspired by a shared interest.

50

chrysanthemums bloom

Prized for their flushes of bright color from late summer through to autumn, chrysanthemums are a welcome reminder that beauty can still be found even as the days are shortening.

In Japan the plants are so highly valued that Chrysanthemum Day, celebrated on the ninth day of the ninth month, is one of the five sacred Japanese festivals. A popular tradition on the festival day is to drink sake, a wine made from fermented rice, infused with chrysanthemum petals. Another custom is to lay cotton wool swabs on chrysanthemum blooms overnight to soak up the dew, then brush them over the face the next day to bring healing powers to the skin.

Remember that beautiful things are waiting around every corner if you take the time to look for them, especially in the natural world where everything flourishes at its own pace.

51

crickets chirp
by the door

**Male crickets chirp for a number of reasons, including
to call other crickets, seduce females, and warn their
enemies to stay away. They make the distinctive noise
using a process called stridulation, which involves rubbing
two of their wings together as a "scrape" and "file."**

As communicators, crickets can teach us a thing or two about speaking up
and not being afraid to say how we feel. Communication is one of the most
important skills we can nurture in order to have successful friendships,
careers, hobbies, and romantic relationships, and there are always ways
to improve. Reflect on your own ability to communicate and ask yourself
if you are open and honest, true to yourself, and willing to share how you
feel with others. If not, try to give yourself more freedom and permission to
speak authentically.

HOW TO HELP THE CONVERSATION FLOW

- Invite someone over for tea, or head out to your local coffee shop and indulge in a slice of cake and a barista-made brew.

- If you struggle to communicate verbally, try writing down your thoughts and feelings on paper.

- Get your mind, body, and soul moving by going for a walk with a friend and sharing your thoughts with every step.

- If you want a good chat with someone, start with the simple question: How are you? Or for something a little different: What is bringing you joy at the moment?

52

frost begins to form

As the temperatures continue to drop and the first frosts form, the landscape appears to go through a magical transformation.

Ice cold to the touch, frost is nonetheless one of nature's most beautiful phenomena, formed when water vapor falls onto a surface cooler than 32°F (0°C), covering it in a blanket of ice crystals. The world becomes a frosty wonderland, like something from a fairy tale, and the long arms of winter begin to take hold of our surroundings. Stillness and quietude drift over the land. Wild creatures retreat into their dens and nests, and the bare bones of trees begin to show as the last of their leaves fall to the earth.

With the return of the first frosts, take this as an invitation from the natural world to find your own form of stillness and quietude. There is nothing to fear in the cold depths of the season—in fact, there is even more beauty to seek out in the form of patterns formed on cold windows, leaves, and stones. Embrace a slow and steady pace where you can, and be mindful of tiny fragments of beauty as you go about your day. Wrap up warm, head outside for a long walk, and surrender to the soft, quiet peace of early winter.

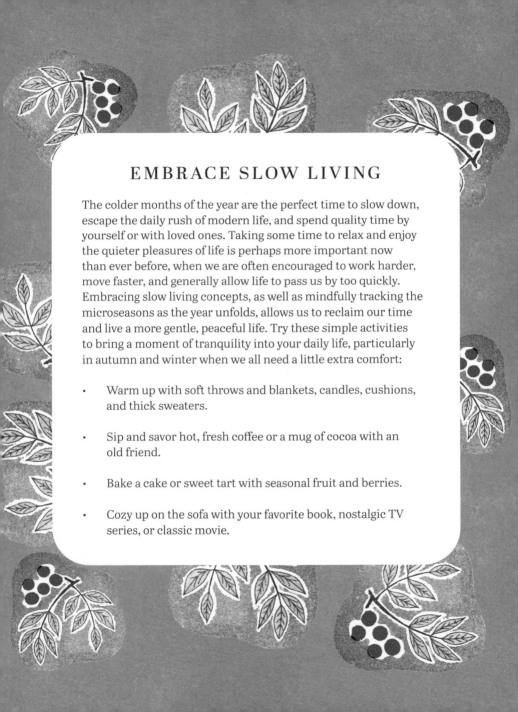

EMBRACE SLOW LIVING

The colder months of the year are the perfect time to slow down, escape the daily rush of modern life, and spend quality time by yourself or with loved ones. Taking some time to relax and enjoy the quieter pleasures of life is perhaps more important now than ever before, when we are often encouraged to work harder, move faster, and generally allow life to pass us by too quickly. Embracing slow living concepts, as well as mindfully tracking the microseasons as the year unfolds, allows us to reclaim our time and live a more gentle, peaceful life. Try these simple activities to bring a moment of tranquility into your daily life, particularly in autumn and winter when we all need a little extra comfort:

- Warm up with soft throws and blankets, candles, cushions, and thick sweaters.

- Sip and savor hot, fresh coffee or a mug of cocoa with an old friend.

- Bake a cake or sweet tart with seasonal fruit and berries.

- Cozy up on the sofa with your favorite book, nostalgic TV series, or classic movie.

53

drizzling rain falls gently

The slow descent into winter is the perfect time to practice mindfulness and meditation, which are both proven to help you relax, de-stress, and cope with the responsibilities of everyday life. This microseason focuses on the drizzling rain of autumn, which you could also take as the inspiration for your own mindfulness practice, using a technique known as the body scan.

A body scan involves focusing intentionally on each part of your body, beginning with the top of your head and moving all the way down to the end of your toes, just like gently falling rain trickling downward. Pay close attention to the feelings and sensations in your body, such as warmth and cold, tension and relaxation, tingling and tickling. How does it feel to inhabit your own body? Which parts of your body do you associate with the most? Celebrate the magic and miraculousness of being alive, feeling the blood pumping through your muscles, the warmth of your life-giving organs, and the strength of your bones.

A healthy body really is something to cherish, so try and feel proud and confident in the one you have. You are a walking, breathing, laughing miracle!

54

maple leaves and ivy turn yellow

Is there anything more breathtaking than the turn of autumn leaves, from bright green to ocher yellow, tangerine, scarlet, and mud brown?

As the darker half of the year creeps in, most deciduous trees will have lost almost all of their leaves. The most beautiful part of the autumn shedding of leaves is the tree's instinctive ability to recognize when it is time to let go of what no longer serves it. Despite putting so much time and energy into the creation of its green foliage, these leaves have now served their purpose and must return to the earth to keep the tree healthy and alive, as well as putting nutrients back into the earth as they rot away, ready to be absorbed through tree roots and turned into brand-new leaves in the future. It is a reminder we all need from time to time, to let go of things that are draining us of resources, even if we have invested time and energy in them beforehand.

Reflect on your own leafy canopy this season, and consider whether there are any parts of your life you would like to let go of in order to keep your own energy levels flourishing. Perhaps a once-glorious friendship has turned slightly toxic, and you need to address how that makes you feel. Or a job you once enjoyed has become miserable and unfulfilling, so a change of career might be on the horizon.

Be honest with yourself and know that only you can decide what will make you happy and healthy.

WINTER

As winter approaches, much of the natural world falls silent, slows down, goes to sleep, or draws from inner resources to keep going through the longest, darkest months of the year. With bare tree branches, shorter days, and lower temperatures, winter can seem hostile and unappealing, but there is still plenty of beauty and wisdom on which we can reflect and meditate, so that we can feel replenished and revived for new growth in the spring.

Winter is the season of deep rest. Not for laziness or boredom, but a time to recharge and sink into the earth, just as the wildflower bulbs hide in the soil until the warmer weather calls them up to the surface. But there is also a sense of newness in the air. The cold, rain, and frost are a blank slate, cleansing the world afresh, and we are given new chances to think differently, try things in new ways, or even to build on existing projects, behaviors, and ideas.

55

camellias begin to bloom

The camellia is an evergreen plant that flowers even in the depths of winter when there is very little sunlight. A symbol of hope, this simple flower can bring us strength as we descend into the dark season, helping to fend off the winter blues that affect us all from time to time.

Is there anything as comforting as a cup of hot, steaming tea on a chilly morning? The leaves of *Camellia sinensis* variants are the main component of a number of everyday teas, including white, yellow, black, green, and oolong. These varieties differ based on the amount of oxidation each undergoes in the preparation of the leaves, creating not only different appearances but subtle changes in flavor, too. Celebrate the blossoming camellia flowers with a tea ritual, allowing yourself to slow down and introspect over a simple, timeless activity.

HOW TO PERFORM
A TEA RITUAL

Use this tea ritual as an opportunity to practice mindfulness and slow down the pace of life. If you can, allow yourself 30 minutes of undisturbed time to practice this ritual. You can choose to enjoy the savoring part of the ritual in a nurturing spot in your home, garden, or a nearby outdoor space. Wrap up warm if it's cold.

1. **Consider.** First decide how you would like to spend your time during the ritual. For example, would you like to simply focus on the moment and savor the smell, taste, and texture of the tea, or would you prefer to read a book, listen to a podcast or music, spend time journaling, or even enjoy a spot of crafting? There is no right or wrong way to perform this ritual—the most important thing is allowing yourself time to focus on inner peace.

2. **Prepare.** Choose your favorite kind of tea blend and preferred utensils for making tea, such as a special mug or teapot. As you begin to boil the water, take some time to check in with how you are feeling. Are there any parts of your body that feel tense or achy? Are there any particular thoughts or worries on your mind? Tune into what your mind, body, and soul are trying to tell you.

3. **Brew.** As the leaves steep in the hot water, close your eyes and breathe in and out, bringing a sense of peace and calm to your mind and body.

4. **Savor.** Once the tea is brewed, focus on the tastes and textures of every sip. What can you see and smell? How does it feel when you first touch the cup to your lips? What memories come to the surface as you sink into the moment?

56

the land begins to freeze

As temperatures fall, the land becomes frosted with ice, and it can seem like the world has entered a kind of stasis, stuck in time.

On a cold, dark day this lack of vibrancy and movement may feel unwelcome, but look closer and discover that the act of slowing down, pausing, or even stopping completely can be a wonderful and important part of survival in the natural world.

HOW TO LEARN FROM
THE NATURAL WORLD

Just as the insects hibernate, the foxes retreat underground, and the trees cast away their unwanted leaves, there are plenty of lessons for us to learn from a frozen world:

- After spending the autumn eating up to 20,000 calories per day, some bears will retreat to their hibernation chambers for winter, drawing on their fat stores to survive. Remember that we can still find inner power even when the outside world is less friendly and accommodating.

- Although butterflies do not technically hibernate, many species will spend the coldest months in a dormant state, finding a sheltered space to be still and conserve energy until the temperature warms up in spring. Most of these will pass the winter as an egg, a chrysalis, or a caterpillar, with the overwintering dormancy a vital part of their growth journey. Remember this when you are next feeling downhearted by the winter stasis—like butterflies, we also need rest and stillness to transform into our best selves.

- Frogs are ectothermic, which means they are unable to generate their own body heat and rely, instead, on their surroundings to keep themselves warm. Some frog species spend the whole winter at the bottom of a pond, hidden among the leaves and mud, which means that, so long as the pond doesn't freeze over and deprive them of oxygen, they will be the first to meet new females arriving in the pond when spring comes. The frog teaches us that even in the wettest, muddiest conditions of winter, nature is still there to nurture us.

57

daffodils bloom

In Japanese culture the daffodil is a symbol of self-love and respect, which echoes the Greek myth with which the daffodil shares its botanical name, *Narcissus*.

According to legend, Narcissus was a figure from Greek mythology who was so impossibly handsome that everyone who saw him fell in love with him. When he shunned the romantic advances of the nymph Echo, the vengeful goddess Nemesis decided to punish Narcissus. One hot day when he was out hunting, he became thirsty and was lured to a pool of water by Nemesis. Within that pool he saw his own reflection and fell so deeply in love with it that he could not leave the pool's side. Unable to accept that his love was not reciprocated, he stayed by the pool until he died, and turned into the white and gold flower we now call the daffodil.

Nobody would benefit from being as self-obsessed as Narcissus, but that doesn't mean we can't learn something from his behavior, particularly when it comes to loving and respecting ourselves. It is much more difficult to care for others and treat them with respect when we cannot do the same for ourselves, so take this microseason as an invitation to celebrate self-love and self-care. Be kind to yourself, cut yourself some slack, and find a way to give yourself a little treat, if you can.

58

rainbows disappear

As the winter days grow shorter there are fewer opportunities for a rainbow to form, which is why the disappearing rainbow has come to be associated with the shift from autumn into winter.

Rainbows appear when light from the sun is reflected and refracted through water droplets suspended in the air, usually just before, during, or after a rain shower. The reflection of the light creates the multicolored arc that has come to be known as a rainbow, but in order for a viewer to see it, the light source needs to be behind them and the light needs to strike the water droplets at a very specific angle. In winter the sun climbs lower in the sky and rainbows are less likely to be seen.

HOW TO CATCH MORE LIGHT

At this time of year, when darkness can seem ever-pressing and the summer sun is a distant memory, look for ways to bring more light into your daily life:

- Wake up early to witness the sunrise, and watch the sun set each evening. Making time to say "hello" and "goodbye" to the daylight will help you soak up every minute of the winter sun.

- When indoors, sit by a window whenever possible to take in as much natural light as you can. You can do this when working at a computer, reading a book, or simply enjoying five minutes of peace with a cup of tea.

- Consider making changes around the lighting design of your home. Do you like bright, dazzling bulbs hanging from the ceiling and lighting up every corner, or do you prefer cozy, muted lamps that create a warm, atmospheric glow? The perfect lighting can transform your living space in winter.

- In the final few hours before bedtime, switch off unnecessary electric lights, strike a match, and light some candles. Enjoy the calming ambience of a dancing flame illuminating the beautiful night that surrounds you.

59

the north wind blows leaves off the trees

Just as the winter winds blast away the last leaves of the season, leaving the branches bare but free of burden, take this opportunity to clear away anything in your life that no longer serves you.

In Japan, a cleaning and decluttering ritual called *osouji*, thought to help banish old ways of thinking and doing and welcome new beginnings, takes place in winter. In practice, this doesn't have to be anything major or life-changing. It could simply be sorting through an untidy corner of the house or cutting back the remnants of summer plants in the garden.

Consider the junk drawer or cupboard of doom. That inoffensive little space housing old receipts, phone chargers, foreign coins, and miscellaneous keys. These small spaces can grow quickly and bring their own micro-doses of stress with them, so do yourself a favor and give yours a clear out.

Spend 15 minutes each week going through the house and gathering up anything that has served its purpose. Whether that's leaflets, takeout menus, or empty wrappers: it's amazing how fast the debris of everyday life can build up.

If you don't need to remove any physical items, treat your home to a deep clean and remove all the dirt and debris from the last 12 months. Pop on a podcast or some music and enjoy the cathartic process of swapping old energy for new.

60

tachibana citrus trees begin to turn yellow

In Japan the tachibana orange (*Citrus tachibana*) is a native variety of wild mandarin that grows in the winter, turning yellow before fully ripening into a bright, vibrant orange color.

Unlike other orange varieties, tachibanas are mostly prized for their smell, not their flavor. The aroma of tachibana peel, released with the lightest scratch, is powerfully zesty, bitter, and tart. In the past, women of the Japanese aristocracy tucked sachets of tachibana blossoms into their kimono sleeves, or threaded the fruits onto cords to wear as perfumed bracelets.

Take this microseason as an invitation to indulge your senses with rich aromas—for example, by using sweet orange essential oil to uplift your spirit with bright, refreshing notes. You could also treat yourself to a new blend of fragrant tea, such as spiced chai (warm, dry, and spicy), green jasmine (rich, floral, and sweet), or Earl Grey (zesty, leafy, and lemony). Fill your home with scented candles and pop a bunch of sweet-smelling flowers on the kitchen table for seasonal joy.

61

the skies stay cold as winter arrives

As the Earth travels around the sun, the hours of daylight decrease until the winter solstice, marked on the shortest day of the year.

These shorter days mean there is less time for the daylight to warm the earth up and more time for the earth to lose heat at night. This leads to the drop in temperature we experience in winter, characterized by ice and snow, cold winds, and a dormant landscape. At this time of year, keep your inner fire glowing against the cold by addressing our most simple human needs.

You don't need to be running marathons in order to keep your body moving through the winter. Slow, steady exercise is the order of the day, such as long walks or yoga—anything to keep the blood pumping.

A cold glass of water might not be the first thing you reach for on a chilly morning, but it's just as important as ever to stay hydrated to fight off winter illness and keep your body functioning well. If you need a little nudge, try sipping decaffeinated or herbal tea.

The winter blues can affect us all, but the most important thing is to keep communicating with loved ones, sharing how you feel, and listening to others. Go for coffee, treat yourself to a night out, or organize a "crafternoon" to enjoy with friends.

62

bears hide away in their dens to hibernate

Technically speaking, there are very few animals that truly hibernate, when the temperature of the body drops to around 32°F (0°C), the heartbeat slows to an almost imperceptible rhythm, and only a few breaths are taken each minute. Animals such as bats, ground squirrels, and groundhogs are considered "true" hibernators, whereas most bears enter a state known as torpor in order to survive the cold winter months.

Torpor is similar to hibernation, but instead of entering one long, deep sleep that lasts until the temperature warms up, torpor is broken up by periods of activity. The bear may wake several times during their winter sleep, usually to give birth, feed, or escape danger. Few of us have the luxury of entering a state of torpor for three months of the year, but we can still channel our inner bears and embrace the magic and tranquility of a good night's sleep.

HOW TO PREPARE FOR SLEEP WITH YOGA

One of the easiest ways to wind down and relax is to practice a couple of simple bedtime yoga moves, using the mattress as a cozy and supportive cushion to help you stretch the day away.

- Cat-cow: Start on all fours with the top of your feet on the bed, your knees directly underneath your hips, and your wrists aligned under your shoulders. For the cat, inhale slowly, then on the exhale, tuck your tailbone under and your chin into your chest, rounding your spine toward the ceiling and pulling your belly button up into your spine. For the cow, inhale slowly while tilting your pelvis forward, lifting your tailbone, chin, and chest to the ceiling, and letting your belly drop and relax. Repeat the cat and cow as many times as you like, transitioning gently between the two.

- Supine twist: Lay face up on the bed and draw your knees into your chest. With your upper body flat, slowly drop your bent legs over to the left, feeling a gentle twist in the right side of your body. For a deeper stretch, press your left hand gently on top of your knees and extend your right arm to the side at shoulder height. Look to the right and hold for several breaths, before switching sides and then repeating.

- Legs-up-the-wall: With your bed against the wall or lying on the floor, sit as close to the wall as you can and lie down on your back, extending your legs up the wall. Place your arms down by your sides or over your head, whichever feels more comfortable to you. Stay in this pose for three to five minutes and focus on your breathing.

63

salmon swim upstream en masse

Salmon are born in freshwater rivers but spend most of their adult lives swimming in the ocean, which means that every year they must return to the place they were born, so they can lay their eggs and ensure the survival of their offspring.

This is a difficult and challenging task. Not only do they lose weight, muscle, and energy by swimming for miles against the currents and over rocks and ledges, but they also face the risk of being eaten by other animals. Those that make it back to their spawning ground do so through a combination of willpower, fitness, and pure luck.

There is an important lesson to be learned from the salmon's journey. Sometimes it can feel like we are swimming upstream for long periods of our lives, fighting obstacles, navigating relationships and jobs, feeling exhausted and, sometimes, hopeless. This is all part of the human experience, and it is important to acknowledge the struggle of darker days, knowing they will end and the balance will be restored. Allow yourself to feel your emotions and, while it is important to keep your head above the water, try not to get trapped in toxic positivity. Some days are better than others, and that is just a part of the beautiful complexity of life. Through challenges and difficulties, we grow as people, and we can almost certainly come out the other side feeling stronger, wiser, and more in tune with ourselves.

64

prunella sprouts

**Even in the depths of winter, the wheel of life continues
to turn, manifested perfectly in the sprouting of the
Prunella plant, also known as common self-heal.**

This medicinally valuable plant is called *utsubogusa* in Japanese, and
although it is difficult to imagine any new life growing in the middle of the
coldest season, it is thought that in southern Japan, where the winters are
milder, small green sprouts of prunella are more likely to appear. Seeing the
fresh green of new plant shoots is one of the best tonics to combat seasonal
sadness, which makes this time of year perfect for planting seeds indoors,
ready for spring.

HOW TO SOW SEEDS IN WINTER

To make room for new seedlings, all you need is a windowsill, as well as a couple of pots, a little soil, and some water, light, and love. See what you can grow this winter!

- Plant delicate, sweet-smelling sweetpeas between autumn and spring on a light, warm windowsill. When the plants are 4in (10cm) tall, pinch out the tips to encourage a bushier growth. Once the frosts have passed, plant them outside and keep them well watered.

- Sow salad leaves indoors in trays or small pots. The seedlings will appear after a few days, and once they have grown into young plants, they can be planted outdoors in containers or directly into the ground.

- Around four to six weeks before the last frost is due, sow cauliflower seeds in trays indoors. Keep the soil moist and the emerging seedlings warm with plenty of sunlight. Transplant outdoors when the roots fill the tray modules.

- Grow salad onions on a sunny windowsill, watering regularly but keeping the soil well drained. Sow small batches every couple of weeks to give you a continual harvest throughout the rest of the year.

- Sow spinach leaves in a warm location with plenty of sunlight. Scatter the seeds thinly over the surface of the soil and lightly press down, so they make a good connection with the soil.

65

deer shed their antlers

In Japanese shamanism, deer are believed to be sacred messengers that carry the gods between this world and the next. One of their most distinguishing features is their antlers, which are made of bone and grow off a pedicle on the top of the deer's head.

Antlers are used by (mostly) male deer to display their health and dominance to the rest of the herd, as well as helping to protect them from predators, knock fruit from trees, and mark their territory by scraping against tree bark. Even though it takes a lot of energy to grow a set of antlers, each year they drop off and are discarded, ready to grow again the following year, a process we can use as a lesson to let go of the things that no longer serve us in our own lives.

There are plenty of things in life that, just like a deer's antlers, have their uses and help us reach a certain point of success or fulfillment. But sometimes the things that were once useful can also become a burden, and it is important to recognize when something is more of a negative presence in your life than a positive one.

HOW TO LET GO

Sit down with a pen and paper and explore these journaling prompts to help you work out what you would like to let go of this season.

- What is something you lose sleep over?

- What are you worrying about that you can't control or change? Why?

- Write about a difficult situation you have overcome.

- Write about your five strongest traits.

- What does letting go mean for you?

- Where would you like to put your energy?

- What are five things that make you happy?

- What are three things you can do right now to make yourself feel better?

66

barley sprouts under the snow

The sprouting barley, one of the world's most important and versatile crops, begins its journey in the depths of winter, ready to rise from the earth and one day reach its final form.

Celebrate the generosity and abundance of the earth, even when so much of it, like the sprouting barley, is hiding beneath layers of winter ice and snow.

There are signs of life everywhere if you look closely enough. Tiny green leaves and shining buds, fresh and new. Stirrings beneath the soil, the smallest movements in the roots of trees. The rays of a soft sun shining down to slowly revive the landscape and bring it back to life. The gentle moon pushing and pulling the ocean's tides, expanding over so much of the earth's surface. There is always something to see, some sign of life that reminds us that the world is still moving, the wheel of the year still turning.

If you can, step outside and look for signs of early growth, from tiny leaflets and newly growing twig buds to the first bright wildflowers of the new season. As you look around at the world, don't forget to look inward, too. What small things are bringing you joy at the moment? What makes you laugh out loud? Focus on the tiny shoots of joy that grow every day.

67

parsley thrives

The Japanese parsley (*Oenanthe javanica*)—or water dropwort—
plant is one of seven herbs that make up a rice porridge dish
known as *nanakusa-gayu*, which is traditionally eaten on
January 7th to mark the end of the new-year celebrations.

After a period of heavy eating, celebration, and indulgence, the *nanakusa-gayu* is valued for its healthy, light ingredients that ease the digestive system back into working order for the new year ahead. The Festival of the Seven Herbs is one of Japan's five annual celebrations, on the morning of which the seven herbs are arranged on a cutting board facing the direction of good luck, before charms are chanted over them. This ritual is said to bring good fortune and health for the coming year to all who partake.

HOW TO MAKE YOUR OWN
NANAKUSA-GAYU

Traditionally, the herbs found in *nanakusa-gayu* include shepherd's purse (*nazuna*); cudweed (*gogyō*); chickweed (*hakobera*); cotton sow thistle (*hotoke gusa*); turnip (*suzuna*); daikon radishes (*suzushiro*); and parsley (*seri*). They are each valued for their medicinal benefits, as well as being delicious and palatable. If these herbs are not easily found in your local area, you could try recreating the dish using easier-to-find alternatives, either from your local landscape or a good-quality grocery store, including watercress, chives, kale, or spinach.

The idea is to nourish your body with simple, healthy food, full of vitamins and minerals, and gentle for an overworked stomach to digest. To make the dish, use rice and water to make a light porridge, then add the chopped herbs with a little salt, dashi, or soy sauce.

If *nanakusa-gayu* doesn't sound like your kind of dish, you can still channel the spirit of a healthy start to the new year with a bowl of soup, bursting with plenty of fresh vegetables, pulses, and good-quality stock.

68

springs once frozen flow once more

Japan is home to around 10 percent of the world's active volcanoes, and hot springs are formed when water bodies in the ground come into contact with molten rock. These springs, known in Japan as *onsen*, have become popular destinations for relaxing, socializing, and reviving the mind and body, particularly to treat stress and fatigue.

The most popular springs are usually located outside beneath open skies, with mineral-rich waters reaching temperatures of almost 122°F (50°C). This microseason refers to the time of year when temperatures drop just enough for the frozen tops of the water to melt, opening up the hot springs below and inviting visitors to sink into their warm, watery depths.

The "snow-watching bath," or *yukimiburo*, is a special experience practiced in Japan's coldest regions, where visitors flock to onsen surrounded by white, sparkling layers of snow. From here they can admire the wintery view while enjoying the hot, therapeutic waters of the volcanic springs beneath them.

While few of us are fortunate enough to have regular access to a hot spring, we can still benefit from the healing properties of the strong contrast between heat and cold. The simplest way is to pour yourself a hot bathtub full of nourishing salts, essential oils, herbs, or seaweeds. Just before you step in, open the bathroom window as wide as you can, so the fresh, winter air can enter the room. Celebrate the heat of the water, soothing and comforting against the body, but also the invigorating nature of the winter air. Inhale it deep into your lungs and feel at peace with the energy of the season.

69

cock pheasants begin to call

The last few weeks of winter mark the beginning of the breeding season for Japan's national bird, the green pheasant. A harbinger of new life ahead, the cock pheasant begins to call at the beginning of the breeding season, paving the way for warmer days, shorter nights, abundance, fertility, and new life.

With their bottle-green feathers and bright red faces, these beautiful birds have featured in Japanese mythology and folklore for centuries, and are even thought to be able to predict geological events like earthquakes. Some believe they are extra sensitive to small movements in the earth that we cannot detect and will "scream" or call out in alert, acting as a natural alarm system. They are also a symbol of harmony due to the way the female pheasant walks together with her chicks.

Channel the positive spirit of these beautiful, green birds by repeating a few of the following positive affirmations in front of the mirror each morning:

I have everything I need to make today a great day.

I am enough, and will always be enough.

Every day, in every way, I am getting better and better.

I am living to my full potential.

70

butterburs put forth buds

The giant butterbur plant (*Petasites japonicus*) produces leaves that are almost 3ft (1m) in width, accompanied by white, creamy flowers that begin to bloom just as the winter season is reaching its end. It takes a lot of energy to create the buds that will grow into these flowers, and doing so during the coldest part of the year can almost seem like an act of bravery for these big, bold plants.

Butterburs symbolize the joy of pushing ourselves out of our comfort zones and trying new things with hope and optimism. Is there something you have been wanting to do, but haven't yet found the courage to start? Perhaps a new hobby you've been meaning to try, a friendship you have wanted to initiate, or a novel you have always wanted to write? Now is the time to think like a giant butterbur and put forth new buds, stretching and challenging yourself in the hope that your actions will evolve into big, beautiful achievements.

HOW TO EXPAND YOUR HORIZONS

If you're feeling stuck for something new to try, how about one of these?

- Join a local evening class or group in your community, particularly to learn a new skill or try something you have never thought of before. If your background is in business or science, why not try a life-drawing class? Or, if you struggle to boil an egg, perhaps you could have a go at French cuisine?

- Learn a new language and plan a trip in the near future to a country where that language is spoken. Start immersing yourself in the culture, listening to podcasts and music in that language, and even making friends with people from your country of choice. Who knows what you may have in common?

- Is there something you have always wanted to do, but never felt confident, skilled, or worthy enough to do it? Perhaps you're interested in writing music, making movies, painting portraits, or becoming a life coach? Take a chance on yourself and have a go. After all, every professional was once an amateur.

71

mountain streams gain a cover of thick ice

Even though spring is edging ever closer, the end of winter can still surprise us with its cold, icy temperatures. This microseason celebrates mountainous regions, where rivers flowing in higher altitudes are exposed to such freezing temperatures and are covered with a layer of ice.

As the last cold weeks of winter drift by, now is the perfect time to reflect on the saying: "No man ever steps in the same river twice, for it is not the same river, nor is it the same man." Mountain streams, icy waters, human footsteps; each of these are laden with their own movement and dynamism, but it is also important to pause and enjoy our journey through the year, one day at a time.

With spring around the corner, it can be tempting to wish time away. But try to find gratitude for even the slowest, coldest winter days. Each one has a message for us, a lesson to learn, a way in which we can develop and improve ourselves, finding fulfillment and tranquility in the beautiful world around us.

HOW TO KEEP A
WILDFLOWER SKETCHBOOK

As the last few weeks of winter fade into spring, now is the perfect
time to tune into your surroundings and look carefully for signs of
the changing season. One of the best ways to do this is by tracking the
emerging wildflowers—some of these will appear as early as midwinter,
while others may take longer, but each one is a reminder of the coming
spring and a new season of growth and rebirth.

Even if you don't consider yourself an "artistic" person, try tracking the
wildflowers with this relaxed sketching exercise. Every time you spot a
new wildflower growing, simply draw your own interpretation of that
flower on a page using any artistic medium you prefer, such as colored
pencils, paints or even a ballpoint pen. Note down the date for each one,
and enjoy the process of documenting the shift from winter to spring
through unique, botanical milestones.

72

hens begin to lay eggs

The laying cycle of an egg-producing chicken is influenced not by the outside temperature, but by the hours of daylight the chicken is exposed to. In the autumn, as the days grow noticeably shorter, chickens begin their annual molt and egg production either slows down or stops completely. As spring approaches and the days begin to lengthen once more, egg production kicks back into gear.

The cause of the connection between egg production and sunlight is the pineal gland, which is activated by light and located just behind the chicken's eye. This gland sends hormones to the chicken's ovaries when enough sunlight passes through the eye, triggering the body to start producing eggs.

This final microseason in the calendar is a wonderful place to end one seasonal cycle and begin another. The last days of winter are ending, and the warmth and brightness of spring brings an abundance of joy and nourishment for the mind, body, and soul. We are only animals, after all, which is why we all share that primitive, instinctive love for sunlight after so many months of heavy, winter weather. As the microseasonal year begins again, find gratitude for every drop of sunlight that reaches you. Meditate on the cyclical nature of our ecosystem, the magical, interconnected web that is fueled by sunshine, oxygen, plants, water, minerals, and atomic matter.

The first egg of spring laid by a healthy chicken is a beautiful symbol of the life force that exists in every corner of our world. Find a moment to appreciate the extraordinary reality of being alive on this planet.

index

Hardie Grant
PUBLISHING

Hardie Grant North America
2912 Telegraph Ave
Berkeley, CA 94705
hardiegrant.com

© 2025 Quarto Publishing Plc

This book was conceived,
designed, and produced by
Quarto Publishing
1 Triptych Place, Second Floor
London SE1 9SH

Assistant Editor: Ella Whiting
Copyeditor: Claire Waite Brown
Illustrator: Tamae Mizukami
Art Director: Martina Calvio
Managing Editor: Emma Harverson
Publisher: Lorraine Dickey
Production manager: David Hearn

Published in the United States by
Hardie Grant North America, an imprint
of Hardie Grant Publishing Pty Ltd.

Library of Congress
Cataloging-in-Publication Data
is available upon request.

ISBN: 978-1-958-41795-9

Printed and bound in China.

First edition.

10   9   8   7   6   5   4   3   2   1

MIX
Paper | Supporting
responsible forestry
FSC® C016973
FSC
www.fsc.org